PRIMARY SOURCES OF THE THIRTEEN COLONIES AND THE LOST COLONY ™

# A Primary Source History of the Colony of
# RHODE ISLAND

## JOAN AXELROD-CONTRADA

rosen central
Primary Source™

The Rosen Publishing Group, Inc., New York

*For Sue and Andrew*

Published in 2006 by The Rosen Publishing Group, Inc.
29 East 21st Street, New York, NY 10010

**Library of Congress Cataloging-in-Publication Data**

Axelrod-Contrada, Joan.
A primary source history of the colony of Rhode Island/Joan Axelrod-Contrada.—1st ed.
    p. cm.—(Primary sources of the thirteen colonies and the Lost Colony)
Includes bibliographical references and index.
ISBN 1-4042-0434-2 (lib. bdg.)
ISBN 1-4042-0675-2 (pbk. bdg.)
1. Rhode Island—History—Colonial period, ca. 1600–1775—Juvenile literature. 2. Rhode Island—History—1775–1865—Juvenile literature. 3. Rhode Island—History—Colonial period, ca. 1600–1775—Sources—Juvenile literature. 4. Rhode Island—History—1775–1865—Sources—Juvenile literature.
I. Title. II. Series.
F82.A98 2006
974.5'02—dc22

                                                                    2005001391

*Manufactured in the United States of America*

**On the cover:** A hand-colored woodcut of Roger Williams building his house in Rhode Island, 1636.

# CONTENTS

# INTRODUCTION

**Independent Spirit**

Rhode Island could be called the Colony of Independent Thinkers. The colony's founder, Roger Williams, believed in the separation of church and state, an idea that the Founding Fathers of the United States would later use to help shape the Constitution. After being banished from Massachusetts for his religious beliefs, Williams announced that his new colony would welcome people of different faiths and viewpoints. Baptists, Quakers, Jews, and others unwelcome elsewhere because of their religious beliefs found a new home in Rhode Island. Relations between the settlers and the native Narragansett tribe got off to a good start, thanks to Williams's respect for the native people.

Rhode Island's original name, the Colony of Rhode Island and Providence Plantations, sheds light on both its history and geography. Geographically, the colony consisted of a large island known as Rhode Island and a mainland called Providence Plantations. Back then, "plantation" meant any kind of settlement, not just the kind of large estate later popular in the Southern colonies.

Before Williams established Providence in 1636, two European navigators explored the coastline of Rhode Island. In 1524, Giovanni da Verrazano, an Italian mariner sailing for France, described a triangular-shaped island in the New World that reminded him of the Greek isle of Rhodes. In 1614, the Dutch explorer Adriaen Block visited an island of red earth that he called Roode Eylandt. The name Rhode Island probably grew out of one or both of those names.

After Williams established Providence, another freethinker named Anne Hutchinson, who was also banished from Massachusetts, started Portsmouth. Hutchinson, a woman unusually bold for her era, was put out of Massachusetts for holding highly opinioned church meetings in her home. Later, another group split off from Portsmouth to found Newport.

In 1663, the colony won a charter from England embodying its ideals of religious freedom. The new seal for the colony bore an anchor and the word "hope." Because of its location by the sea, the colony developed shipbuilding and other maritime pursuits.

For much of the 1600s and 1700s, Newport surpassed Providence in both population and importance. Newport's bustling port attracted pirates, privateers, and merchants. Around this time, Rhode Island got the nickname Rogue's Island for its tolerance of pirates. Finally, after England threatened to withdraw its charter in the early 1700s, Rhode Island started punishing pirates.

In the 1700s, many Rhode Island merchants took part in the lucrative slave trade. Although it might seem odd that a colony founded on the freedom of individuals would profit off the enslavement of others, many of Rhode Island's independent-minded merchants valued profits above all else. Rhode Island's Quakers, on the other hand, took a firm stand against slavery.

In the 1760s and 1770s, independent-minded Rhode Island played a leading role in opposing British rule. Its residents organized an act of defiance known as the Gaspee Affair that rivaled the actions of the later Boston Tea Party. In 1772, Rhode Island patriots burned the *Gaspee*, a British ship, and shot its captain. Three years later, Rhode Island held its own "tea party."

Then, on May 4, 1776, Rhode Island proclaimed its independence from British rule two months before the nation's leaders signed the Declaration of Independence. But, when it came to joining the new United States government, Rhode Island once again showed its independence. Afraid of losing the rights guaranteed under its charter, Rhode Island became the last of the thirteen states to join the new union.

To this day, Rhode Island celebrates the spirit of religious and political freedom that harks back to Roger Williams. Atop the capitol building stands a statue known as the Independent Man. In the 1780s, the nation's Founding Fathers made ideas similar to Williams's about religious freedom the law of the land. The Bill of Rights proclaims that the government "shall make no law respecting an establishment of religion, or prohibiting the free exercise thereof." In doing so, the spirit of colonial Rhode Island continues to this day.

# CHAPTER 1

## Roger Williams's Providence

One January day in 1636, an independent-minded minister named Roger Williams got some unsettling news. Massachusetts's authorities were coming to arrest him. They wanted to send him back to England.

Williams fled into the wilderness with at least one of his followers, Thomas Angell, heading south toward Narragansett Bay. They trudged through the snow and ice, scavenging for nuts and berries to survive. Finally, they reached Williams's Native American friends in what is now Rhode Island.

Three months earlier, a Massachusetts court had found Williams guilty of spreading "dangerous opinons." Although the Puritans had come to Massachusetts to worship as they pleased, they set up a government as intolerant of religious diversity as the Church of England had been. Williams believed in the separation of church and state, an idea that was radical for its time. From the moment he arrived in Massachusetts in 1631 with his wife, Mary, Williams caused a stir. Some people even considered him a heretic.

Once in Plymouth, Williams shocked authorities by calling into question the king's right to grant land to the colonists. The land, he said, belonged to the Native Americans. If the colonists wanted land, they needed to negotiate with the Native Americans for it.

Finally, in Salem, Williams irritated authorities by arguing that it was wrong to punish people for religious crimes such as fishing on the Sabbath. He also took issue with an oath that included the words "so help me God." Williams later wrote, "Forced worship

Roger Williams (1603–1683) fled England and founded the colony of Rhode Island in 1636, with the goal of promoting religious freedom for himself and his followers. Although his desire to keep matters of religion and government separate was considered radical in the 1600s, American leaders later embraced the idea of a separation between church and state. For this reason, many people consider Williams among the fathers of American democracy. This contemporary charcoal drawing of Williams was created in 1964. There were no portraits done of Williams during his lifetime.

stinks in God's nostrils," according to Amy Allison in *Roger Williams: Founder of Rhode Island*.

Massachusetts authorities summoned Williams to court and tried to get him to soften his beliefs. Williams refused. On October 9, 1635, the court issued its decree: "Whereas, Mr. Roger Williams, one of the elders of the church of Salem, hath broached and divulged diverse new and dangerous opinions . . . it is therefore ordered that the said Mr. Williams shall depart out of the jurisdiction within six weeks."

Soon after the decision, Williams became severely ill and asked the court to allow him to stay until the spring. The court agreed as long as he kept quiet about his ideas. Williams, however, could not keep silent. In January, authorities came to arrest him, but he had fled into the wilderness three days earlier with at least one of his followers.

After he was exiled from the Massachusetts Bay Colony for his "new and dangerous opinions" Williams used this compass and sundial to guide him and Thomas Angell during their fourteen-week journey through the wilderness to Narragansett Bay. After he purchased the land that would later become Rhode Island from the Narragansett Indians, he named the colony Providence to thank God for his survival.

Although his exact route remains unknown, Williams probably used his compass and sundial to guide him. He later wrote that he wandered for fourteen weeks, "not knowing what bed or bread did mean." His journey led him to land controlled by the Wampanoag and Narragansett Indians. Williams knew the Native Americans from his days as a missionary and trader in Salem and Plymouth.

Williams and Angell eventually settled on land controlled by the Narragansett tribe. According to Emily Easton in the book *Roger Williams: Prophet and Pioneer*, a group of friendly Native Americans greeted Williams in his canoe by calling out, "What cheer, netop?" (*netop* means "friend," and "what cheer" was the common English greeting of the period). The Native Americans then treated him and his fellow traveler to a dinner of boiled bass and succotash.

The two Narragansett chiefs, Canonicus and his nephew Miantonomi, gave Williams land to start a new settlement. According to Easton, Williams later drew up a deed for the land stating that the chiefs gave it to him as a gift for his "many kindnesses and services." Over the years, Williams had shown his friendship to the chiefs by giving them gifts of sugar and other highly valued items. Canonicus signed the agreement by drawing a bow, and Miantonomi by drawing an arrow, since the Native Americans lacked a written language.

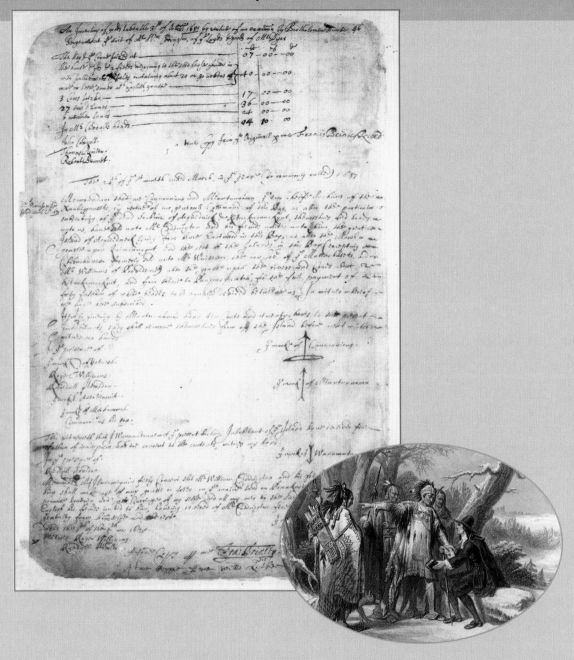

This handwritten page *(left)* is a copy of the original deed of the Providence colony in Rhode Island. Although the main purpose of the document was to record the purchase of land, the transfer of other items such as farm animals is also included. Note the marks made by the Narragansett chiefs Canonicus and Miantonomi in 1637, who signed their names with symbols, because they lacked a written language. The nineteenth-century print *(right)* features a group of Narragansett Indians assisting Roger Williams upon his arrival in the Narragansett Bay area.

Williams named his new settlement Providence, a word referring to God's guidance. He sent for his wife and two daughters in Salem and announced that Providence would welcome people of all religious backgrounds.

At first the settlers lived in huts similar to the Native Americans' wigwams. Williams divided the land into equal-sized parcels for settlers. Each settler got five acres (2 hectares) for a garden and six acres (2.4 hectares) for cornfields. The settlers caught fish and hunted game. Because British coins were scarce, townspeople used goods such as corn or strings of Indian shells known as wampum to pay for goods.

Williams wrote to his old friend from Massachusetts, Governor John Winthrop, about the joys and difficulties of starting a new settlement. In a letter dated October 24, 1636, he addressed Winthrop as "Much Honoured Sir." "I confess my gains counted up in man's exchange are loss of friends, esteem, maintenance, etc.," he wrote.

That same fall, Winthrop wrote back to Williams, asking him to break up a possible alliance between the Narragansett and Pequot tribes. The Pequot wanted to unite the Native Americans against the colonists. Winthrop knew that no one could communicate with the Native Americans like Williams could.

Williams put aside any resentment he might have felt toward Massachusetts and convinced the Narragansett not to join forces with the Pequot. And when war broke out in 1637, the Narragansett instead fought on the side of the colonists. On the night of May 25, the colonists, along with their Narragansett allies, set fire to a Pequot village in Connecticut. They had ignored Williams's earlier pleas to spare the lives of the Native American women and children. The remaining members of the Pequot tribes fled. Shortly thereafter, the Narragansett were so disgusted and horrified by the scope of the killing that the war ended.

Because Roger Williams had a long-standing and peaceful relationship with the Narragansett Indians (and spoke many Indian languages), the governor of the Massachusetts Bay Colony, John Winthrop, requested Williams's help in breaking up a potential alliance between Narragansett and Pequot tribes in 1636. Tensions between the Pequot and some European settlers escalated into a war the following year, and, possibly in part because of their relationship with Williams, the Narragansetts fought alongside the colonists. In this eighteenth-century print, English settlers are fighting alongside the Narragansett in 1637.

Providence established its own government without any help or support from England. On August 20, 1637, the settlers signed a paper known as the Providence Agreement. The phrase "only in civil things" showed that government in Rhode Island would be separate from all religious practices.

Meanwhile, back in Puritan Massachusetts, people continued to be punished for religious offenses, such as missing church or swearing. Some of the most famous of these rebels would soon find their way to Rhode Island.

# CHAPTER 2

**T**wo years after Roger Williams founded Providence in 1636, another group of religious rebels from Massachusetts arrived in Rhode Island. Anne Marbury Hutchinson, an outspoken woman, had gotten into trouble with Massachusetts authorities for holding prayer meetings in her Boston home. A middle-aged midwife and mother of twelve, Hutchinson believed that faith alone was not enough to ensure salvation. In Hutchinson's opinion, people did not need to follow church rules in order to be saved.

## New Settlements

Not surprisingly, authorities viewed Hutchinson as a threat to the colony. In November 1637, they summoned her to appear before the general court. Hutchinson defended herself brilliantly, citing passages from the Bible to justify her prayer meetings. But then she lost her temper, and the justices turned against her.

In the court's decision, Governor Winthrop announced, "You are banished out of our jurisdiction as being a woman not fit for our society." The forty-six-year-old Hutchinson was put under house arrest until her sentencing on March 15, 1638.

While she was under house arrest, a group of her followers in Boston signed an agreement to organize themselves into a political body and start a new settlement. This document, signed on March 7, 1638, came to be known as the Portsmouth Compact. Signers included Hutchinson's husband, William, as well as the group's leader, William Coddington, and his friend Dr. John Clarke, a physician.

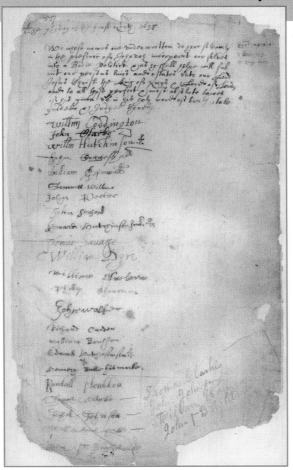

While outspoken religious leader Anne Marbury Hutchinson (1591–1643) was found guilty of being a heretic in the Puritan courts of the Massachusetts Bay Colony, her followers were already discussing the formation of a new settlement outside of Massachusetts. The Portsmouth Compact (also known as the Aquidneck Compact) was a civil agreement between Hutchinson's followers to start a new independent colony. It was written on March 7, 1638, and signed by nineteen of Hutchinson's followers. For a transcription of the agreement, see page 54.

The wealthy and ambitious Coddington originally planned to lead the group to Delaware. But, after meeting up with Williams in Providence, he settled on Rhode Island. Williams helped Coddington and his friends negotiate a deed with the Narragansett chiefs for a parcel of land. The chiefs gave the new settlers land on Aquidneck Island (later renamed Rhode Island) in exchange for wampum and tools. Settlers called the new town Pocasset but soon changed its name to Portsmouth.

Hutchinson then joined her followers in Portsmouth after her sentencing left her excommunicated from the Boston church and banished from Massachusetts. The trip from Boston was a difficult one, as Hutchinson was pregnant at the time. Upon

Anne Marbury Hutchinson, an educated woman whose father was also silenced for his religious beliefs, is pictured in this nineteenth-century illustration during her trial in the Massachusetts Bay Colony. Unlike the Massachusetts Puritans, Hutchinson believed that spirituality was an experience unique to the individual. In 1637, she was found guilty for "traducing [slandering] the ministers" in the colony and was forever banished from it. With the desire for religious freedom, she and her followers founded Portsmouth, Rhode Island, in 1638.

arrival, she lived in a dugout covered with tree bark while her husband built a wood-frame house for the family. Still, even with great care, Hutchinson's baby was stillborn.

Town meetings in Portsmouth quickly became heated. Although Coddington had supported Hutchinson in Boston, he disagreed with her in Portsmouth. He was the more conservative and ambitious of the two. In 1639, Coddington and Dr. Clarke left Portsmouth to start their own settlement on the other side of Aquidneck Island. They named the new settlement Newport. In 1640, realizing they needed the strength of collaboration and unity, Portsmouth and Newport formed a joint government.

Yet another exile from Portsmouth founded Rhode Island's fourth town, Warwick. Samuel Gorton, an opinionated and hot-tempered man, did not believe in heaven or hell. He started a religious sect of members called Gortonites. Gorton and his followers got into trouble wherever they went.

In Portsmouth, Gorton insulted justices by calling them "just-asses." Then, in Providence, one of Gorton's followers refused to pay his debt. Town representatives came to take the man's cow as a form of payment, but Gortonites fought them off with pitchforks. Gorton eventually bought land from Miantonomi and two lesser chiefs to found a settlement in 1643 that he called Shawomet. But after the two chiefs complained they had not gotten their fair share of wampum, Massachusetts authorities decided to intervene. In the fall of that year, some forty soldiers from Massachusetts came to arrest Gorton and bring him to Boston to stand trial. Once there, officials questioned him about his religious practices, found him guilty of blasphemy, and sentenced him to jail for the winter of 1643 to 1644.

After serving his sentence, Gorton sailed to England in the spring of 1644 to get permission to return to Shawomet. The Earl of Warwick helped him get his wish. To show his appreciation, Gorton renamed the settlement Warwick.

Williams saw Massachusetts's meddling in the Gorton affair as proof that the Narragansett settlements needed their own charter. A charter would show that the settlements were legal in England's eyes. In 1643, Massachusetts, Plymouth, New Haven, and Connecticut had banded together to form the United Colonies without inviting Providence and the surrounding settlements. Williams worried that the United Colonies would try to gobble up the rest of southern New England unless he got a charter for Warwick, Newport, and Portsmouth.

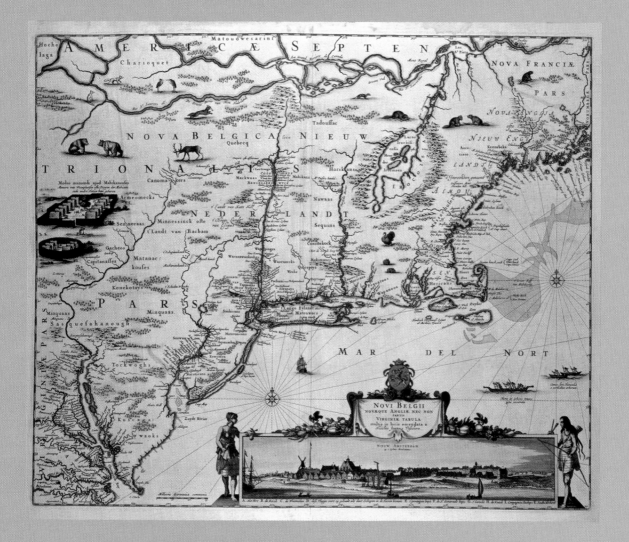

The Dutch colony of New Netherland is featured along with New England on this seventeenth-century map of the region. Justus Danckerts created this watercolor map in 1651, after a composite map by Nicolaes Visscher. It remains among the most lavishly decorated maps of the period that feature Rhode Island. Like most maps from this era, it was made to encourage Europeans to settle in New Netherland.

In the spring of 1643, Williams set sail for London. While on the ship, he wrote his famous book, *A Key into the Language of America*, about Narragansett culture, language, and way of life.

In his book, Williams presented the Native Americans as equal to, if not superior to, the Europeans. "Boast not, proud English, of thy birth and blood," he wrote. "Thy brother Indian is by birth as good." Williams was particularly impressed by the Native Americans' hospitality. The Narragansett had no beggars or fatherless children like were then seen on the streets of London.

On March 14, 1644, Parliament granted Williams his charter. The agreement gave settlers in the Providence Plantations of Providence, Portsmouth, and Newport the right to "govern and rule themselves by such forms of civil government by voluntary consent of all, or the greater part of them." (Warwick was added to the charter in 1647.) It also protected the colony from invasion or takeover by its neighbors.

Williams then returned home, welcomed by a fleet of decorated canoes. Together, townspeople celebrated the new charter. Williams traveled from town to town to unify the colony while setting up a trading post to supplement his income. He and his wife now had six children to support. At first, he refrained from selling alcohol because he thought some Europeans might use it to take advantage of the Native Americans. After a while, though, he decided to sell "a little wine or strong water to some natives in theare [their] sickness."

On May 18, 1647, representatives from Providence, Portsmouth, Newport, and Warwick met to establish a central government. The form of government was to be "Democratical."

The ambitious William Coddington, however, refused to celebrate the new charter. He wanted more power for himself. His old rival, Anne Hutchinson, had left Portsmouth for upstate New York (then controlled by the Dutch) in 1642. With her gone, Coddington worked to make Aquidneck a separate colony with himself governor for life.

In 1649, Coddington sailed to England to get his plan approved. Parliament gave him what he wanted. He had succeeded in dividing the colony in two. People wondered how this could have happened. They expected that the charter of 1644 would protect the unity of the settlements.

After news of the division reached Williams, he sold his trading post to pay for another trip to London. Dr. John Clarke, who also disapproved of Coddington's actions, accompanied Williams on the voyage. On October 2, 1652, the two men got an order reaffirming the 1644 charter.

Unity had been preserved. In 1656, as is printed in the *Dictionary of American Biography,* Coddington admitted his defeat. "I, William Coddington, doe freely submit to ye authority of his Highness in this colony as it is now united and that with all my heart."

# CHAPTER 3

**Growth and Conflict**

Rhode Island's promise of religious freedom attracted new settlers to the colony. People unwanted elsewhere— Baptists, Quakers, and Jews, among them—were welcomed in Rhode Island.

In 1639, Roger Williams helped start the first Baptist church, an offshoot of Puritanism in America. Baptists believed that only adults should be baptized. Within a year Williams left the Baptist church to become a Seeker, someone who sought his own spiritual truth without belonging to any organized church.

In 1657, Quakers settled in Rhode Island. The Quakers believed in following an "inner light." In Massachusetts, the nonviolent Quakers irked authorities by refusing to take part in skirmishes against the Native Americans. Because of their commitment to nonviolence, Quakers were whipped, banished, and sometimes executed. Quakers who returned to Massachusetts after being expelled could have one or both of their ears cut off. In time, many Quakers fled to Rhode Island for safety.

In 1658, a group of Jews of Spanish and Portuguese descent arrived by boat in Newport. Williams, who served as president of the colony, welcomed them eagerly. These early Jewish settlers purchased a plot of land for a cemetery, the oldest existing Jewish cemetery in the United States. In 1763, a second wave of Jewish immigrants opened the Touro Synagogue, the oldest surviving synagogue in the United States.

Outsiders scoffed at Rhode Island's diverse mix of people. The colony, they said, harbored riffraff. A Connecticut minister

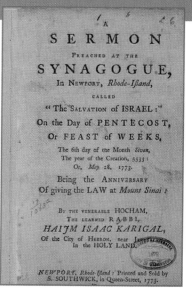

While many religious groups were treated as outcasts in seventeenth-century New England, Rhode Island was a colony where people could worship as they pleased without fear of prejudice or hatred. Among the religious groups who found refuge in Rhode Island were the Jews, who built the Jeshuat Israel Synagogue in 1763. This postcard *(left)* shows an image of the synagogue from 1910. On the right is the title page of a Jewish sermon given in Rhode Island in 1773. For a transcription, see page 55.

compared Rhode Island to a "sink" where other colonies could dump their religious waste. The United Colonies of Massachusetts and Connecticut demanded that Rhode Island expel its Quakers. But Williams refused. "They [Quakers] have their liberty amongst us, are entertayned [sic] into our houses, or into any of our assemblies," the Rhode Island Assembly maintained.

Meanwhile, political changes in England again threatened Rhode Island's charter. King Charles II declared that he would undo all the legislation passed in the government before him, including the charter for Providence Plantations. At this news, Dr.

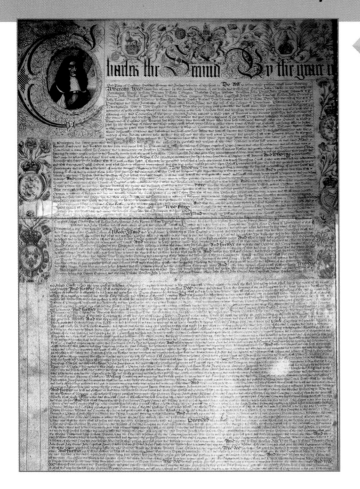

Various settlements in Rhode Island continued to separate from Roger Williams's original colony, mostly due to the desire of various groups to worship individually. When the United Colonies of Massachusetts and Connecticut demanded that Quakers be removed from Rhode Island, a new charter that guaranteed freedom of religious expression was sought from England's King Charles II. According to a book written by Henry William Elson in 1904, Rhode Island, along with Connecticut, enjoyed more freedom than any other colony. For an excerpt from the 1663 charter, see page 55.

John Clarke of Newport worked to negotiate another charter for the colony.

In 1663, Clarke obtained a new charter from King Charles II providing for a democratic government and complete religious freedom in Rhode Island. The charter proclaimed the continuation of a "lively experiment."

On November 24, 1663, townspeople gathered at Newport for a public reading of the charter. It was lifted out of its case so everyone could see the magnificent document with its majestic seal. Townspeople listened to its stirring words read aloud, granting Rhode Islanders the right "to hold forth a lively experiment that a most flourishing civil state may stand and best be maintained with full liberty in religious concernments."

The charter allowed Rhode Island more self-rule than any other colony. Male property owners would elect their own governor rather than have one appointed by the king. However, the colony of Rhode Island and Providence Plantations, as it was now called, limited the rights of some of its residents. Catholics and Jews could worship freely, for example, but they were not yet permitted to vote.

While settlers in Rhode Island saw hope in their future, Native Americans felt a growing sense of despair. Europeans were increasingly taking over their lands. Some New Englanders used tricks such as getting Native Americans drunk on liquor—what they called "strong water"—so Native Americans would sign away their rights more easily.

Meanwhile, in Massachusetts, tensions had also increased between settlers and the Wampanoag Indians. Chief Massasoit, who had befriended the Pilgrims, was dead. Massasoit's eldest son had died mysteriously after being questioned by Plymouth Colony officials. The younger son, Metacomet, suspected his brother had been poisoned.

Metacomet, who was called King Philip by the colonists, organized an alliance of tribes to fight the colonists. War broke out in June 1675. Although Rhode Island tried to stay neutral, it was drawn into the conflict that winter.

Some historians believe that the problems began after the Narragansett Indians agreed to let the Wampanoag women and children stay at their winter camp to protect them from the war. The United Colonies demanded that the Narragansetts turn over their Wampanoag guests. The Narragansetts refused because their culture called for hospitality. The United Colonies issued a final warning, then prepared for attack.

On December 19, 1675, the New England army stormed a Narragansett village. Only a few Rhode Island colonists joined the army, which consisted mostly of men from Massachusetts Bay, Plymouth, and Connecticut. The colonial troops attacked during a heavy snowstorm, setting off one of the bloodiest massacres in history. Blood stained the snow red as the colonists set the village on fire. Altogether, about 1,000 Native American men, women, and children were killed in the Great Swamp Fight.

Soon after the bloody conflict, an unnamed colonist wrote an account of it for publication in London. Told strictly from the English point of view, the piece blamed the conflict on the "quarrelsome disposition" of the "barbarous and savage Indian natives," according to *A Further Brief and True Narration of the Great Swamp Fight in the Narragansett Country*. The colonists needed to kill them in order to restore peace, it said. The account ended with a list of the English slain and wounded in battle.

Soon after, the Native Americans regrouped. The Narragansetts joined the Wampanoags in attacks on many European settlements in both Massachusetts and Rhode Island. In the spring of 1676, Native Americans prepared to attack Providence.

By this time, both of the Narragansett chiefs who had befriended Roger Williams were dead. Canonicus, who was like a father to Williams, had died in 1647, at about the age of eighty. His nephew, Miantonomi, was slain in 1643 by a Mohegan chief, at the behest of the Massachusetts colonial authorities. In 1676, Miantonomi's son Canonchet became chief.

Williams, who was about seventy-three years old at the time, limped out to meet the young chief. For an hour, he tried to convince Canonchet not to attack Providence. Unfortunately the chief had already made up his mind. Williams, however, would be

Roger Williams witnessed the burning of Providence by Native Americans in 1675, which included his home, seen here in an idealized print. Although Newport was spared from destruction, to Williams, who remained unharmed during the incident because of his long-standing relationships with Native Americans, the conflict had erased decades of progress.

spared, according to the same account, "You have been kind to us many years," one of the Narragansetts told him. "Not a hair of your head shall be touched."

The Native Americans did not hurt Williams, but they burned down half the town, including Williams's home. He went to live with his son while the colonial militia set out to capture King Philip.

A spy passed along the information that King Philip liked to sleep on a huge rock in Rhode Island. On the morning of August

12, 1676, the colonial forces waited to ambush Philip. When he woke up, he found himself surrounded. A Native American fighting on the side of the colonists shot King Philip to death.

With King Philip dead, the war ground to a halt. It had taken a toll on both sides. Both Warwick and Providence were destroyed. Thousands of Narragansetts and Wampanoags had been killed, as had many other Native Americans who had come to colonial missionary-sponsored "praying towns."

For the Europeans, the end of King Philip's War meant they could build new settlements on land that once belonged to the Native Americans. Between 1676 and 1700, the population of Rhode Island nearly doubled. New towns such as Pawtucket, Bristol, East Greenwich, Kingston, Westerly, Woonsocket, and Cranston were soon established.

Most families lived in simple homes with few frills. Settlers ate food similar to that of the Native Americans—game, corn, and squash—using plates and utensils made out of wood. When people made their wills, they mentioned their most prized possessions, such as a cow or perhaps a feather bed.

Williams remained active in Providence affairs until his death in 1683. His death marked the passing of an era. Before one assembly in Providence in 1680, he questioned the legality of a meeting called without the required "three days warning." He showed the same kind of concern for the rules of the town as he had for freedom of religion. In the years ahead, democratic principles in Rhode Island would become less important than making a profit.

# CHAPTER 4

## To the Sea

As the 1700s dawned in Rhode Island, the colony prospered. Farmers produced enough surplus goods to export some for profit. Newport became a bustling center of trade. Many Rhode Islanders found new opportunities as sailors, merchants, and even pirates.

Between the mid-1600s and the mid-1700s, England fought the Netherlands in a series of wars at sea. The British government hired colonists as privateers to attack Dutch ships. The privateers then raided the ships for treasures to sell back home. One advertisement for privateers read, "All Gentlemen Sailors and Others have now a fine Opportunity to distinguish themselves and make their Fortunes."

Many privateers doubled as pirates. In between wars, they attacked ships for themselves rather than for the British government. Some were so successful they became full-time pirates. At one point, Rhode Island harbored so many pirates it became known as Rogue's Island. Captain William Kidd of Scotland sometimes sought refuge among his friends in Rhode Island. The famous Captain Kidd was rumored to have buried treasure on Block Island, an island off the coast of Rhode Island that was first settled by the English in the 1660s.

Rhode Island also had its own pirates. Thomas Tew of Newport was known for his distinctive pirate flag that featured a hand clasping a sword. Fellow seaman William Mayes Jr., eventually left behind his life of robbing ships to take over his father's tavern. The White Horse Tavern, founded in 1673, is the oldest continuously operating tavern in the nation. Mayes was granted a license in 1702 to sell "all sorts of Strong Drink."

Although pirates are often romanticized, their illegal gains at sea made them criminals. They often bribed Rhode Island officials to look the other way. Finally, Rhode Island governor Samuel Cranston decided to take action against the pirates. He wanted to appease English officials and rid the colony of some of its undesirables. On July 19, 1723, in front of a huge crowd, twenty-six pirates were hanged outside of Newport.

Piracy gave way to other, more legitimate ventures at sea. Merchants traveled around to the farm towns to collect lumber, butter, cheese, and livestock to export. Rhode Island farmers raised a special breed of horses called Narragansett Pacers, which were valued throughout the colonies for their speed.

Other Rhode Islanders turned to fishing and whaling. In the late 1740s, a Jewish merchant named Jacob Rodriguez Rivera began making candles from the oil of sperm whales. In Providence, the prominent firm of Nicholas Brown and Company sold spermaceti candles with a label featuring a whale. Before long, more than a dozen candle-making shops sprang up in Newport.

By the mid-1700s, most Rhode Islanders were involved either directly or indirectly in trade of some sort. Beginning in 1710, the colony released paper currency to facilitate trading. New jobs increased around the ports. Ships needed clerks to keep records, coopers to build barrels, stevedores to carry the heavy barrels on board, and, of course, sailors. Wealthy merchants belonged to the Newport Marine Society.

But Rhode Island's merchants found slave trading to be the most profitable of all maritime endeavors. Many Rhode Islanders took part in the Triangular Trade, which linked the American colonies to the West Indies and Africa. Rhode Island merchants bought sugar and molasses in the West Indies, which they made

Many of Rhode Island's sailors etched images into the teeth and bones of the whales they caught as a colonial pastime. This nineteenth-century example of scrimshaw, a decorated jawbone of a whale, is typical of those done earlier. Whales were the source of many colonial commodities including candles, lamp oil, tools, hardware fittings, and sewing needles. The teeth of sperm whale were especially popular for scrimshaw because they could be highly polished and then tinted to accentuate the detail of the carving.

into rum. By 1750, Newport alone had twenty-three distilleries busily turning molasses into rum. The merchants then used the rum to buy slaves in Africa.

Slave trading was a risky business. Sometimes slaves died of disease, took their own lives, or rebelled. An article in the *Providence Gazette* on July 11, 1763, chronicled the journey of a slave ship wracked by a storm and rebellion:

It is impossible to describe the Misery the poor Slaves underwent, having had no fresh Water or Food for [five]

Days. Their dismal Cries and Shreiks [sic], and most dismal Looks, added a great Deal to our Misfortunes; four of them were found dead, and one drowned herself in the Hold.

Providence merchant Nicholas Brown and his brothers John, Joseph, and Moses had a similar experience with their ship, the *Sally*, in 1765. Disease and rebellion ravaged the population of the *Sally*. Moses Brown became a leading opponent of slavery even though his brother John continued in the slave-trading business.

Slaves who survived the long, treacherous journey in good health sold for the highest prices. An advertisement in the *Providence Gazette* on Saturday, June 11, 1762, announced the upcoming auction of "Twenty-three fine, healthy Slaves, just arrived from the Coast of Africa."

Slave trading was profitable enough to absorb the periodic losses from disease and revolt. Many wealthy Rhode Islanders saw nothing wrong with using slaves. A typical help-wanted ad appeared August 7, 1773, in the *Providence Gazette*:

WANTED, A NEGRO Fellow, from [sixteen] to [twenty-five] Years of Age, or even [thirty] free from bad Smell, straight-limbed, active, healthy, good-tempered, honest, sober, quick at Apprehension, and not used to run away. A good Price with be given, and the money paid immediately. Enquire at the Printer.

Some slaves escaped. An ad appeared in the *Providence Gazette* on May 14, 1768, describing one runaway: "about [twenty-four] years of Age, a likely, well built Fellow, has had the

Quakers, consistently opposed to violence and slavery, began freeing their slaves in 1773. This document from 1784, page 124 of the Acts & Resolves of the Rhode Island General Assembly, 1783–1784, Volume 23, authorized the "manumission of Negroes, Mulattos & Others and for the gradual abolition of slavery" throughout Rhode Island. In many cases, slaves were guaranteed their freedom after they reached adulthood at the age of eighteen.

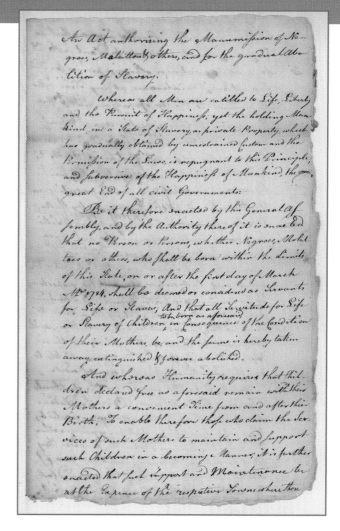

Small-Pox, and talks bad English; had on when he went away a blue strait-bodied Shag Coat and a Jacket cuffed with red Shag."A reward was offered for his capture.

As the 1700s wore on, Rhode Islanders became increasingly opposed to slavery. Many Quakers freed their own slaves in a process known as manumission. One freed black started a music school. Another became a caterer. Towns now had paved roads and a variety of shops and businesses. Rhode Island was no longer a wilderness.

# CHAPTER 5

## Daily Life in the 1700s

Everyday life in colonial Rhode Island could be either simple or grand, depending on one's circumstances. While most Rhode Islanders lived simple, self-sufficient lives, the wealthy often had servants and slaves. In the South County, large farmers known as Narragansett Planters presided over plantations similar to those of the Southern colonies. They relied on slave labor to raise the livestock, grow the crops, and make the dairy products they exported.

Many merchants of Newport also kept slaves. Some slaves wore wigs and expensive uniforms to reflect the status of their masters. From 1740 until 1770, Newport enjoyed a period of prosperity known as its golden age. Providence ranked a distant second in population and importance.

Newport's top merchants lived in luxurious, well-decorated homes. Their wealth trickled down to the talented furniture makers, portrait painters, silversmiths, seamstresses, and shopkeepers who kept them in style. Portrait painter Gilbert Stuart got his first commissions as a teenager in Newport, then went on to paint a series of portraits of America's first president, George Washington. Newport's elite belonged to exclusive clubs and attended dance recitals, poetry readings, and theatrical performances. Taverns entertained visitors with lavish food, dancing, and card games.

Both George Washington and Benjamin Franklin visited Newport at this time. During his visit in February 1756, Washington was a twenty-four-year-old colonel en route from

This eighteenth-century mahogany bureau table, attributed to the carpentry shop of John Townsend, is a testament to the rich craftsmanship of Rhode Island's artisans. Though many residents of the young colony struggled, others lived in well-decorated homes rich with opulent furnishings and accessories. At the time, Rhode Island was a leader of American furniture production dominated in part by the Townsend and Goddard families.

Boston to New York to meet with the head of British forces in America. While in Newport, he broke a bowl belonging to the wealthy merchant Godfrey Malbone. Washington promptly sent $8 in Virginia currency to repay Malbone for his loss.

Franklin first came to Rhode Island to visit his older brother, James, who owned a printing press in Newport. James Franklin started the first newspaper in Rhode Island in 1732, but it lasted less than a year. His son, also named James, had better luck. The younger James Franklin launched the *Newport Mercury* in 1758.

Brown University is pictured above as it appeared in 1795 in this reproduction print from 1945. Brown University was originally founded in 1765 as Rhode Island College. The school moved to Providence in 1770 and was renamed in 1804 for Nicholas Brown, an American manufacturer and philanthropist who graduated from its halls in 1786.

Providence got its own newspaper four years later. A widow named Sarah Updike Goddard provided the money for her son, William Goddard, to start the newspaper *Providence Gazette and Country Journal*. But in 1766, William Goddard decided to move to Philadelphia. He turned the newspaper over to his mother and sister, who were highly educated for women of that era.

Rhode Island lacked a public school system until after the colonial period. Unlike Massachusetts, which used its public school system to help bring about religious uniformity, Rhode Island saw less of a need for mandatory education. In Rhode Island, families who wanted an education for their children needed to teach them themselves or pay for it. Private dame schools sprang up in the homes of women (also called dames) to teach young children basic reading and arithmetic. Families also paid private tutors to educate their children.

In 1764, Rhode Island opened its first college in Warren. When Rhode Island College was forced to relocate, both Providence and Newport offered it a home. Providence won out in 1770, thanks to the generosity of merchant Nicholas Brown. The college changed its name to Brown University in 1804 to show its appreciation. Like other colleges of the day, it accepted only boys.

Girls were expected to stay home and help their mothers with the cooking, sewing, weaving, and other handicrafts. Women in colonial Rhode Island cooked over a big fire. Rhode Island became famous for a special kind of cornmeal pancakes known as journey cakes because they were often eaten on trips. Over the years, journey cakes became known as jonny cakes or Johnny cakes.

Millers, who ground the corn into cornmeal for the Johnny cakes, set up shop in town alongside carpenters, shoemakers, potters, blacksmiths, and other artisans. Workers billed customers for their labor. Stonecutters, for instance, charged for the number of letters and decorations on gravestones. Teenage boys typically learned a craft by apprenticing. They lived with a master who provided room, board, and instruction in return for labor.

But life wasn't all work. Men frequented taverns to socialize, eat, drink, and play card games. Women often combined work and pleasure in quilting bees, spinning bees, and the like. Children played cricket and other games after tending to their chores.

Not all households were happy ones, however. Newspapers frequently carried ads from subscribers whose wives or

This document is among the colonial records of the Newport Historical Society. It is one accounting page from 1728, from the notebooks of John Stevens, a stonemason. Stevens's *Commonplace Book*, as it later came to be known, was where he recorded a variety of facts such as the price of goods, lists of books he read, his favorite verses, and information about his business accounts. The entries span from 1705 to 1768, around the same time Stevens worked installing marble hearths, cutting holes in grindstones, and creating gravestones.

apprentices had run away. One spurned husband took out an ad in the *Providence Gazette* in 1762, freeing himself of all financial responsibilities for his runaway wife. Another subscriber to the *Providence Gazette* offered a reward for the return of a fifteen-year-old apprentice named William whose face was "a little seamed with the Small-Pox." The smallpox virus caused a rash that scarred the skin and was frequently fatal. A few physicians advertised their services in local newspapers, but their remedies often caused more harm than good.

Newspapers of the day also carried news about local events. Before long, the news focused on the growing tensions between England and the thirteen colonies. Rhode Island soon became one of the first colonies to openly rebel against England.

# CHAPTER 6

## Rebellion Against the British

For years, Rhode Island and England got along peacefully by ignoring each other. As it was written in its charter, England allowed Rhode Island to govern itself. Although British laws extended to colonial trade, they were rarely enforced. Rhode Islanders became masters at smuggling illegal goods to the colony while British officials looked the other way.

But in the 1760s, all that changed. England had just waged the expensive French and Indian War (1754–1763) against France. Parliament decided that the colonies should help pay off some its war debts, so in 1764, a new law called the Sugar Act was passed calling for duties on imported molasses and sugar. Because Rhode Island's livelihood rested largely on the molasses trade, the colony strongly opposed the legislation.

Rhode Islanders also objected to the Stamp Act, a tax on newspapers and other paper goods, about to be passed by Parliament. At the time, Stephen Hopkins, the governor of Rhode Island, took a strong stand against England's new policies. In November 1764, he published an influential pamphlet called *The Rights of Colonies Examined* (also called *The Grievances of the American Colonies Candidly Examined*). In it, he argued that the colonists were to "receive protection, and enjoy all the rights and privileges of free-born Englishmen." His pamphlet helped raise the cry of "No taxation without representation!"

Newspapers also helped stir up public opinion in favor of rebellion against England. On August 24, 1765, William Goddard

To the right is the title page of a pamphlet written by Stephen Hopkins (1707–1785) in December 1764 called *The Rights of Colonies Examined*. Widely published soon after in newspapers such as the *Providence Gazette*, Hopkins wrote the piece in response to Parliament's newly imposed Sugar and Stamp Acts. Hopkins was a self-educated man who became governor of Rhode Island, a political leader in the fight for American independence, and a signer of the Declaration of Independence. Recognized as a great patriot, Hopkins's gravestone reads, in part, "Here lies the man in fateful hour, who boldly stemmed tyrannic power. And held his hand in that decree, which bade America be free!"

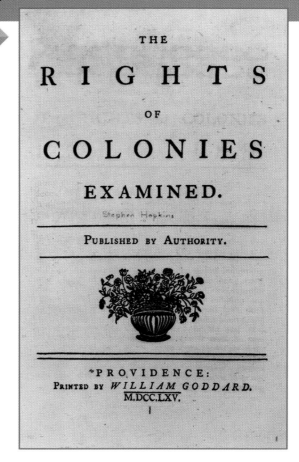

published a special issue of the *Providence Gazette* that included a chart showing how much the costs of everyday items would increase as a result of the Stamp Act.

Americans throughout the colonies protested the Stamp Act, which took effect on November 1, 1765. At the same time, England appointed Americans as stamp masters to enforce the unpopular law. In Newport, opponents of the Stamp Act hanged and burned dummies made to look like the stamp master and two of his Tory (pro-British) allies. The mob then destroyed the homes of the two Tories. They spared the home of the stamp master because he resigned, leaving the position empty.

THE BOSTONIANS PAYING THE EXCISEMAN, OR TARRING AND FEATHERING.

Colonial outrage against the Stamp Act of 1765 was widespread. Protests, both published in newspapers and heard in public gatherings, were common. Colonists resisted the harshly imposed tax by boycotting British goods, refusing to use stamps or stamped paper, and forming opposition groups such as the Sons of Liberty. In this political cartoon, Bostonians can be seen forcing tea down the throat of a tax collector whom they have tarred and feathered in protest of the hated Stamp Act.

No one else wanted to enforce the law. Nor did shopkeepers and court officers want to implement the new system. Newspapers went out as usual without stamps. The Rhode Island General Assembly sided with the Stamp Act opponents by declaring that the citizens of Rhode Island need not obey any laws other than their own.

In early 1766, Parliament repealed the Stamp Act. Rhode Islanders fired cannons and rang church bells across the colony to celebrate, but the fanfare was short-lived. The British passed new tax laws, which the angered Americans also disobeyed.

On January 11, 1768, the *Newport Mercury* published an article comparing "enslavement" by Parliament to American slavery. The writer argued that the only way to prevent slavery from abroad was to stop "that hellish practice of deluding and enslaving another part of the human species, I mean Negroes."

In the next few years, sentiment against the British grew among both blacks and whites. In response, Americans throughout the colonies voted to boycott British goods. Many Rhode Islanders promised to forgo British woolens for homespun cloth. Women organized knitting circles and spinning bees to meet the increased demand.

In Newport, however, some merchants refused to honor the boycott. They wanted to be free to trade with whomever they chose. Other colonies reacted angrily by threatening to cut off trade with Rhode Island. Finally, the merchants agreed to support the boycott.

Rhode Island also became a leader in attacks on British ships. Rhode Island's burning of the British ship the *Gaspee* in 1772 rivaled Massachusetts's Boston Tea Party as a dramatic act of rebellion.

The *Gaspee*, a British ship assigned to stop smuggling in Narragansett Bay, became a much-hated presence in Rhode Island waters. Rhode Islanders particularly disliked the ship's captain, William Dudingston, for his rigorous enforcement of tax laws. On June 10, 1772, a group of Rhode Island patriots raided the *Gaspee*. In the scuffle that followed, a young patriot shot Dudingston. A Rhode Island doctor treated the wound, and Dudingston recovered. Once everyone was off the vessel, the patriots burned it.

The British government responded to the *Gaspee* affair by launching an official inquiry. Burning a British ship was a crime punishable by death. The British offered a reward for information about the destruction of the *Gaspee*, but no one ever claimed the reward. Rhode Islanders refused to testify against each another. In the end, no one was ever punished for the incident, and the

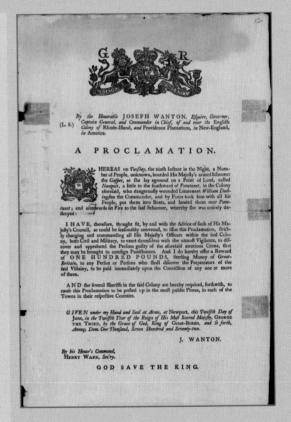

Charles Dewolfe Bramnell painted this image *(above)* of the British sailing vessel *Gaspee*, showing the ship as it exploded off the coast of Rhode Island on June 10, 1772. Colonists had long been irritated at the British, who had been collecting taxes and harassing colonial vessels in Rhode Island's harbor. To get even, colonists decided to strike the schooner after it had run aground off the coast of Providence in a place called Namquid Point (now called Gaspee Point). With the intention of destroying the ship, hundreds of colonists boarded small boats, paddled out to the *Gaspee*, exchanged gunfire with the British, and proceeded to ignite the hull. Within moments the entire ship exploded. Although King George III posted an award *(right)*, no person was ever charged with a crime. For an excerpt of the proclamation, see page 56.

British acknowledged that the colonists had been provoked by overly strict enforcement of the rules.

As recounted in *The History of Bristol, Rhode Island*, by W. H. Munro, Thomas Swan, a participant in the *Gaspee* affair, wrote a song about the incident. It began:

Twas in the reign of George the Third,
Our public peace was much disturbed
By ship of war that came and laid,
Within our ports, to stop our trade.

Opposition to the British heated up again in 1773 and 1774. After Parliament passed the Tea Act in 1773, Boston staged its famous Boston Tea Party. The following year, the Rhode Island General Assembly called for all the colonies to come together in a Continental Congress. With the urging of Rhode Island representative Stephen Hopkins, the First Continental Congress voted to establish a navy as well as an army.

As anti-British sentiment spread, so, too, did opposition to slavery. In 1774, Rhode Island passed a law forbidding the importation of slaves into the colony.

Then, in March 1775, Providence held its own "tea party." Unlike the Boston Tea Party, which was staged in secret by a small group, Providence's affair was open to the public. The tea-burning celebration took place in the market square. As recorded by Peter Force in *A Documentary History of the Origin and Progress of the North American Colonies*, the town crier announced:

All true friends of their country, lovers of Freedom, and haters of shackles and hand-cuffs are hereby invited to testify their good disposition, by bringing in and casting into the fire, a needless herb, which for a long time has been detrimental to our liberty, interest, and health.

Participants threw not only tea but also pro-British speeches and newspapers into the fire. While it burned, a spirited member of the Sons of Liberty went up and down the street, painting out the word "tea" on shop signs.

On April 19, 1775, patriots faced off against British troops in the Battle of Lexington in Massachusetts. The Revolutionary War had begun.

The following spring, Rhode Island made history by declaring its independence from Great Britain two months before the rest of the country. On May 4, 1776, the Rhode Island General Assembly passed a resolution repealing its allegiance to British rule. This came two months before the Second Continental Congress approved the historic Declaration of Independence on July 4, 1776. The colonies, however, would need to win the Revolutionary War for that to happen. And at first, that didn't seem likely.

# CHAPTER 7

A merica's long conflict for independence turned many Rhode Island men into soldiers and sailors during the Revolutionary War. Stephen Hopkins's younger brother Esek became commander of the new Continental navy. Esek Hopkins soon found himself with a difficult job. Rhode Island sailors shied away from the navy because they preferred the higher profits and looser discipline of privateering. Unable to recruit enough volunteers, Hopkins was dismissed from his position.

# The Thirteenth State

Army commander in chief George Washington managed to survive his trial under fire, although he, too, found himself in a difficult position. The Continental Congress had little money to spend on soldiers. Many went barefoot and hungry. One delegate to the Continental Congress worried that men were trading their clothes for liquor. Disgusted by the lack of food and supplies, many soldiers deserted.

The *Providence Gazette* carried ads offering rewards for deserters. In an ad that appeared on April 27, 1776, Captain Asa Kimball offered a $5 reward for a soldier named Nicholas Shippee, who was "very much given to liquor."

On December 8, 1776, the horrors of war hit home when seventy-six British ships invaded Newport. British troops occupied Newport for the next three years, prompting half the people to flee to Providence. Neighboring Connecticut sent in food and supplies to prevent a crisis. The once magnificent city of Newport became an empty shell. The British roamed over the island, burning houses for firewood and slaughtering the livestock of local farmers.

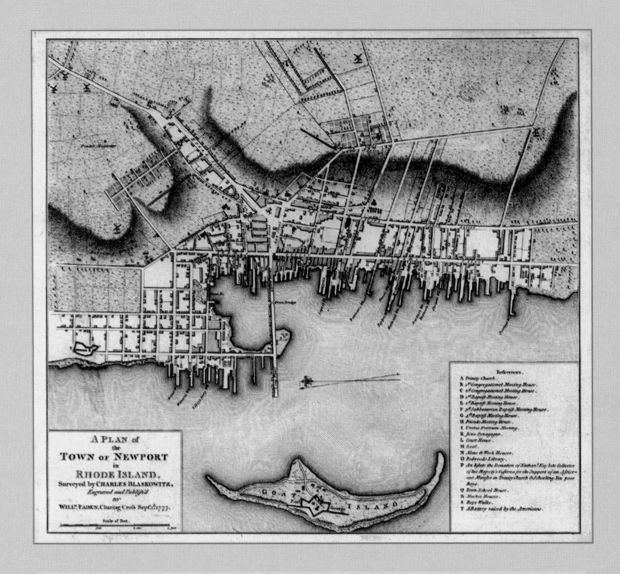

Englishman William Faden created this hand-colored map of Newport, Rhode Island, in 1777, probably for the benefit of the British soldiers who were stationed there during the Revolutionary War. Among the items referenced on the map are the various houses of worship for religious groups that were prevalent in Newport at the time, including Catholics, Congregationalists, Baptists, Quakers, and Jews.

Many who remained in Newport sided with the British. In some cases, family members differed in their loyalties. Mary Gould Almy, for instance, sided with the British while her husband served in the American army. According to Elizabeth Evans in *Weathering the Storm: Women of the American Revolution*, in a letter to her husband, she expressed her dislike for "the nation that you call your friends." She kept busy by renting rooms to boarders.

At first, George Washington was too busy with other battles to make winning back Newport a priority. Then, in early 1778, France entered the war on the side of the Americans. Washington approved a plan for a coordinated attack on Newport. American troops would attack the British in Newport from the east while a French fleet would enter from the west. The American force included Rhode Island's Black Regiment, which was formed after the General Assembly approved a plan to purchase slaves and set them free if they agreed to serve in the army.

In the summer of 1778, the American and French fleets headed for Newport. A storm, however, prompted the French troops to turn back. The abandoned Americans retreated to Portsmouth, where they came upon the British. On August 29, 1778, the two sides fought the Battle of Rhode Island.

Colonel Israel Angell wrote about the battle in his diary on August 29, 1778. "I had three or four men kill'd and wounded to day at night," he wrote. "I had not Slept then in two nights more than two or three hours [and] the Reg[iment] had eat[en] nothing during the whole Day this was our situation to go on guard, but we marched off Chearfully [sic] and took our post."

After winning the battle, the British continued to occupy Newport for the next year. In October 1779, they left on their own accord to join in the battles taking place to the south.

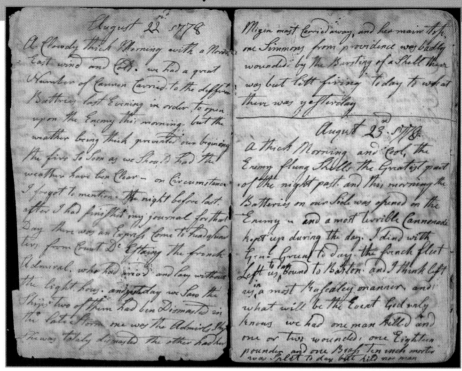

Above is a page dated 1778, from the diary of Israel Angell (1740–1832), descendent of Thomas Angell, who was among the first residents of Providence and a follower of Roger Williams. During the American Revolution, Israel Angell was a commander in the Continental army, where he led attacks during the Battles of Brandywine, Red Bank, and Monmouth. He was also stationed in Valley Forge under General George Washington during the winter of 1777 to 1778. His distinguished military career was further decorated by his valor during the Battle of Springfield in Rhode Island on June 23, 1780.

By 1780, American troops had developed the organization needed to defeat the British, largely due to the efforts of a general from Rhode Island named Nathanael Greene. A trusted confidant of George Washington, Greene had grown up in a Quaker family but was expelled because of his volunteer military efforts. He skillfully solved the problem of getting supplies to the soldiers by building roads and obtaining horses and wagons. He also helped orchestrate the Battle of Yorktown in 1781, which resulted in the

General Nathanael Greene (1742–1786), pictured in this engraving from 1785, was among the first settlers of Rhode Island. A dear friend of General George Washington, Greene distinguished himself in the Revolutionary War by recapturing the South from British control. Before entering the military, Greene had served in Rhode Island's General Assembly.

surrender of the British. The Revolutionary War was over. On September 3, 1783, Great Britain and America signed the Treaty of Paris. Great Britain acknowledged the birth of a new nation, the United States of America.

With the war over, Rhode Island became one of thirteen states under a weak central government created by the Continental Congress. Providence emerged as the state's new commercial center since Newport was ravaged by war. The postwar years brought a period of economic depression, with paper money becoming almost worthless compared to gold. These years also brought debates at both the national and state level about slavery. In 1784, the Rhode Island General Assembly passed a law calling for the gradual emancipation of slaves.

By 1787, many Americans recognized the need for a stronger central government to maintain order and boost the economy.

prefent convention, America may yet enjoy peace—lately—liberty and glory.

HARRINGTON.

❖❖❖❖❖❖❖❖❖❖❖❖❖❖❖❖

PORTSMOUTH, (New Hampfhire) May 19.
We are authorifed to inform our readers that the probability of the honorable delegates from this ftate not attending the convention at Philadelphia, caufes great uneafinefs in the minds of the true whigs of New Hampfhire, and will occafion a confiderable infpection into the ftate of our finances.

Near one quarter part of the towns in this ftate have refolved not to fend any reprefentatives to the enfuing General Court. A correfpondent fuppofes this circumftance will greatly accelerate public bufinefs.

BOSTON; May 19.
The legiflature of Connecticut having laft week appointed its deputies, twelve ftates will be reprefented in the grand federal Convention, now fitting in Philadelphia.—Rhode Ifland is the delinquent ftate—but, obferves a correfpondent, this is a circumftance far more joyous than grievous; for her

This notice dated May 30, 1787, told Philadelphia readers that Rhode Island was the only state not represented during the Constitutional Convention of May 1787. Fearing that the state would lose its independence and the rights of its residents, Rhode Island refrained from its support of the new Constitution until 1790.

Rhode Island, however, remained as independent-minded as ever. When a young man named Alexander Hamilton invited the thirteen states to send delegates to a convention in Philadelphia to form a stronger union, Rhode Island ignored his call. The national convention held in Philadelphia from May to September 1787 created a new set of laws for the nation called the Constitution.

Over the next two years, every state but Rhode Island approved the Constitution. Rhode Islanders argued against joining the new federal government because they worried that the state would lose its independence and be overshadowed by the larger states. Rhode Islanders also wanted to guarantee the rights of individuals. Once Congress created a Bill of Rights, Rhode Islanders were more in favor of the new government. The First Amendment embodied the principles Roger Williams set forth about the separation of church and state. Finally, in May 1790, a Rhode Island convention voted to approve the Constitution. Rhode Island then became the thirteenth state of the United States.

In August 1790, President George Washington visited Rhode Island to welcome it into the Union. Rhode Island greeted Washington with huge crowds and much fanfare. Church bells rang, and cannons sounded. In Newport, the president stayed in the boardinghouse run by former Loyalist Mary Gould Almy. During his stay, he wrote a stirring letter to the members of the Touro Synagogue affirming the principles upon which Rhode Island was founded, according to Evans's *Weathering the Storm*:

> The Citizens of the United States of America have a right to applaud themselves for giving to Mankind examples of an enlarge and liberal policy, [one] worthy of imitation. All possess alike liberty of conscience and immunities of citizenship," Washington wrote. Rhode Island, the colony of the independent minded, had become a model for the nation.

# TIMELINE

1636 — Roger Williams flees Massachusetts and founds Providence.

1638 — Anne Hutchinson and followers establish Portsmouth.

1639 — Williams founds first Baptist church in America.

1644 — Williams receives charter for Providence Plantations.

1654 — Williams is elected president of the combined colonies of Providence, Newport, Narragansett, and Warwick.

1657 — First Quakers settle in Rhode Island.

1658 — First Jews settle in Rhode Island.

July 8, — New charter proclaims continuation of a "lively
1663       experiment."

1675-- Great Swamp Fight and the burning of
1676      Providence; King Philip's War is fought between colonists and Native Americans.

1694 — Rhode Island General Assembly authorizes privateers for King William's War between England and France.

| | |
|---|---|
| July 19, 1723 | — Twenty-six pirates are hanged outside of Newport, putting an end to the age of piracy. |
| 1764 | — Rhode Island College (later renamed Brown University) is founded. |
| June 10, 1772 | — American patriots burn the British ship *Gaspee*. |
| May 4, 1776 | — Rhode Island proclaims its independence from Great Britain two months before the rest of the colonies do. |
| August 29, 1778 | — Battle of Rhode Island is fought near Portsmouth. |
| 1784 | — Rhode Island Emancipation Act provides for gradual elimination of slavery. |
| May 29, 1790 | — Rhode Island approves U.S. Constitution and becomes the thirteenth state. |

# PRIMARY SOURCE TRANSCRIPTIONS

**Page 14: The Portsmouth Compact (also known as the Aquidneck Compact)**

**Transcription**
The 7th Day of the First Month, 1638.

We whose names are underwritten do hereby solemnly in the presence of Jehovah incorporate ourselves into a body politic and as He shall help, will submit our persons, lives and estates unto our Lord Jesus Christ, the King of Kings, and Lord of Lords, and to all those perfect and most absolute laws of His given in His Holy Word of truth, to be guided and judged thereby. [In the margins are the following Bible citations: Exodus 24:3-4, II Chronicles 11:3, II Kings 11:17].

William Coddington
John Clarke
William Hutchinson, Jr.
John Coggeshall
William Aspinwall
Samuel Wilbore
John Porter
John Sanford
Edward Hutchinson, Jr. Esq.
Thomas Savage
William Dyre
William Freeborne
Phillip Shearman
John Walker
Richard Carder
William Baulston
Edward Hutchinson, Sr.
Henry Bull
Randall Holden

**Page 21: Excerpt from a sermon preached at the Jeshmat Israel Synagogue in Newport, Rhode Island, called "The Salvation of Israel"**

## Transcription

On the Day of Pentecost, Or Feast of Weeks, The [sixth] day of the Month Sivan, The year of the Creation, 5533: Or May 28, 1773. Being the Anniversary of giving the LAW at Mount Sinai: By the venerable Hocham, The Learned Rabbi, Haijm Isaac Karigal, Of the city of Hebron, near Jerusalem, In the Holy Land . . .

**Page 22: Excerpt from the Royal Charter for Rhode Island, granted by King Charles II and adopted July 8, 1663**

## Transcription

CHARLES the Second, by the Grace of God, King of England, Scotland, France and Ireland, Defender of the Faith, &c., to all to whom these presents shall come, greeting:

Whereas, we have been informed, by the petition of our trusty and well-beloved subject, John Clarke, on the behalf of Benjamin Arnold, William Brenton, William Codington, Nicholas Easton, William Boulston, John Porter, John Smith, Samuel Gorton, John Weeks, Roger Williams, Thomas Olney, Gregory Dexter, John Coggeshall, Joseph Clarke, Randall Holden, John Greene, John Roome, Samuel Wildbore, William Field, James Barker, Richard Tew, Thomas Harris, and William Dyre, and the rest of the purchasers and free inhabitants of our island, called Rhode Island, and the rest of the colony of Providence Plantations, in the Narragansett Bay, in New England, in America, that they, pursuing, with peaceable and loyal minds, their sober, serious, and religious intentions, of godly edifying themselves, and one another, in the holy Christian faith and worship, as they were persuaded; together with the gaining over and conversion of the poor ignorant Indian natives, in those parts of America, to the sincere profession and obedience of the same faith and worship, did, not only by the consent and good encourage-ment of our royal progenitors, transport themselves out of this kingdom of England into America, but also, since their arrival there, after their first settlement among other our subjects in those parts, for the avoiding of discord, and those many evils which were likely to ensure upon some of those subjects not being able to bear, in these remote parts, their different apprehensions in religious con-cernments, and in pursuance of the aforesaid ends, did once again leave their desirable stations and habitations, and with excessive labor and travel, hazard and charge did transplant themselves into the midst of the Indian natives, who as we are informed, are the most potent princes and people of all that country; where, by the good Providence of God, from whom the Plantations have taken their name, upon their labor and industry, they have not only been preserved to admiration, but have increased and prospered, and are seized and possessed, by purchase and consent of the said natives, to their full content, of such lands, islands, rivers, harbors and roads, as are very convenient, both for plantations, and also for building of ships, supply of pipe-staves, and other merchandise; and which lie very [rich in commodities], in many respects, for commerce, and to accommodate our southern plantations, and may much advance the trade of this our realm, and greatly enlarge the territories thereof; they having by near neighborhood to and friendly society with the great body of the Narragansett Indians, given them encouragement of their own accord, to subject themselves, their people and lands, unto us; whereby, as is hoped, there may, in time, by the blessing of God upon their endeavors be laid a sure foundation of happiness to all America. And whereas, in their humble address, they have freely declared, that it is much on their hearts (if they may be permitted) to hold forth a lively experiment, that a most flourishing civil state may stand and best be maintained, and that among our English subjects, with a full liberty in religious concerns; and that true piety rightly grounded upon gospel principles, will give the best and greatest security to sovereignty, and will lay in the hearts of men the strongest obligations to true loyalty . . .

## Page 42: Excerpt of the Proclamation by King George III

### Transcription

. . . Whereas on Tuesday, the ninth [omitted word] in the Night, a Number of People, unknown, boarded His Majesty's armed Schooner the Gaspee, as she lay aground on a Point of Land, called Nanquit, a little to the southward of Pawtuxet, in the Colony aforesaid, who dangerously wounded Lieutenant William Dudingston the Commander, and by Force took him with all his People, put them onto Boats, and landed them near Pawtuxet; and afterwards set Fire to the said Schooner, whereby she was entirely destroyed:

I HAVE, therefore, thought fit, by and with the Advice of such of His Majesty's Council, as could be feasibly convened, to issue this Proclamation, strictly charging and commanding all His Majesty's Officers within the said Colony, both Civil and Military, to exert themselves with the utmost of Vigilance, to discover and apprehend the Persons guilty of aforesaid atrocious Crime, that they may be brought to [omitted word] punishment. And I do hereby offer a Reward of ONE HUNDRED POUNDS, Sterling Money of Great Britain, to any Person or Persons who shall discover the Perpetrators of the said Villainy, to be paid immediately upon the Conviction of any one or more of them . . .

# GLOSSARY

**banish** To drive away.

**blasphemy** A show of disrespect toward God.

**broach** To raise or bring up in conversation.

**charter** A document granted by a king or queen that grants certain rights to a body of people.

**civil** Governed by the state as opposed to military or religious authorities.

**colony** A group of people who settle in a distant land but are governed by the mother country.

**constitution** A code of principles or laws forming a government.

**deserter** Someone who leaves the armed forces without permission.

**divulge** To make public.

**emancipation** The act of setting free.

**heretic** One who holds opinions that differ from established beliefs, especially religious beliefs.

**hospitality** The warm and friendly treatment of strangers or guests.

**Johnny cake** Originally "journey cake"; a cornmeal pancake often eaten on journeys.

**jurisdiction** The territory over which a particular government has control.

**livestock** Animals kept on a farm or raised for sale and profit.

**manumission** The act of being freed from slavery by one's owner.

**maritime** Having to do with the sea.

**merchant** A person whose business is buying and selling goods.

**midwife** Someone who assists in childbirth.

**missionary** One who spreads a religion to people of different beliefs.

**molasses** A dark syrup produced in making sugar.

**pirate** Someone who attacks and robs ships without government approval.

**privateer** A person hired by a government to attack and rob enemy ships.

**riffraff** People who are considered no more valuable than trash.

**rum** An alcoholic drink made from molasses.

**salvation** The act of saving or being saved.

**scrimshaw** A carving or engraving done on ivory, animal bone, seashells, or antlers.

**sect** A group of people that form a distinct unit within a larger group by virtue of common beliefs.

**smallpox** A highly infectious virus characterized by a high fever and rash.

**smuggle** To transport goods secretly to avoid paying customs dues.

**stevedore** A person in charge of loading and unloading ships.

**tavern** A place that serves liquor.

**town crier** A person who shouts out announcements for the town.

**traduce** To slander or defame.

**triangular trade** A system that links three countries in a continuous flow of trade. During colonial times, a triangular trade system linked Europe, Africa, and the New World. For example, molasses was brought from the West Indies to Rhode Island, where it was transformed into rum, which would then be traded in Africa for slaves. Slaves were then transported back to the New World, where they would be sold in Rhode Island or in other colonies.

**wampum** Small shell beads used as money by Native Americans.

# FOR MORE INFORMATION

Gaspee Days Committee
P. O. Box 1772
Pilgrim Station
Warwick, RI 02888
(404) 781-1772
Web site: http://www. gaspee.com

The Newport Historical Society
82 Touro Street
Newport, RI 02840
(401) 846-0813
Web site: http://www.newporthistorical.com

The Rhode Island Historical Society
110 Benevolent Street
Providence, RI 02906
(401) 331-8575
Web site: http://www.rihs.org

Roger Williams National Memorial (National Park Service)
282 North Main Street
Providence, RI 02903
Web site: http://www. nps.gov/rowi

## Web Sites

Due to the changing nature of Internet links, the Rosen Publishing Group, Inc., has developed an online list of Web sites related to the subject of this book. This site is updated regularly. Please use this link to access the list:

http://www.rosenlinks.com/pstc/rhis

# FOR FURTHER READING

Allison, Amy. *Roger Williams: Founder of Rhode Island.* Philadelphia, PA: Chelsea House, 2001.

Doherty, Kieran. *Puritans, Pilgrims, and Merchants: Founders of the Northeastern Colonies.* Minneapolis, MN: The Oliver Press, 1999.

Kling, Andrew. *The Thirteen Colonies: Rhode Island.* San Diego, CA: Lucent Books, Inc., 2002.

McCarthy, Pat. *The Thirteen Colonies: From Founding to Revolution.* Berkeley Heights, NJ: Enslow Publishers, Inc., 2004.

Wroble, Lisa A. *Kids in Colonial Times.* New York, NY: The Rosen Publishing Group, 1997.

# BIBLIOGRAPHY

Angell, Israel. *Diary of Colonel Israel Angell Commanding the Second Rhode Island Continental Regiments During the American Revolution 1778-1781* (reprint). New York, NY: The New York Times & Arno Press, 1971.

Beals, Carleton. *Colonial Rhode Island.* Camden, NJ: Thomas Nelson, Inc., 1970.

Easton, Emily. *Roger Williams: Prophet and Pioneer.* Boston, MA: Houghton Mifflin, 1930.

Evans, Elizabeth. *Weathering the Storm: Women of the American Revolution.* New York, NY: Charles Scribner's Sons, 1975.

*A Further Brief and True Narration of the Great Swamp Fight in the Narragansett Country*, Society of Colonial Wars in the State of Rhode Island and Providence Plantations, 1912 reprint of book published in London in 1676.

Gaustad, Edwin S. *Roger Williams: Prophet of Liberty.* New York, NY: Oxford University Press, 2001.

Hedges, James B. *The Browns of Providence Plantations, Colonial Years.* Cambridge, MA: Harvard University Press, 1952.

Hopkins, Stephen. *The Rights of Colonies Examined.* Providence, RI: The Rhode Island Bicentennial Foundation, 1974.

Lippincott, Bertram. *Indians, Privateers, and High Society: A Rhode Island Sampler.* New York, NY: J. B. Lippincott Company, 1961.

Lovejoy, David S. *Rhode Island Politics and the American Revolution, 1760-1776.* Providence, RI: Brown University Press, 1958.

McLoughlin, William G. *Rhode Island: A Bicentennial History.* New York, NY: W. W. Norton & Company, Inc., 1978.

Taylor, Maureen Alice. *Runaways, Deserters, and Notorious Villains from Rhode Island Newspapers Volume I: The Providence Gazette, 1762-1800.* Rockport, ME: Picton Press, 1994.

Winslow, Ola Elizabeth. *Master Roger Williams: A Biography.* New York, NY: The MacMillan Company, 1957.

# PRIMARY SOURCE IMAGE LIST

**Page 9:** Compass and sundial owned by Roger Williams, circa 1630, creator unknown. Brass. Decorative Arts Museum Collection: 1902.3.1. In the collection of the Rhode Island Historical Society in Providence, Rhode Island.

**Page 10:** The Deed of Providence, dated March 24, 1637, housed in the Department of Colony Records 1646-1669, in the Rhode Island State Archives.

**Page 14:** The Portsmouth Compact (also known as the Aquidneck Compact) of 1638. Housed in the Rhode Island State Archives.

**Page 17:** Justus Danckerts created this watercolor map in 1651, after a composite map by Nicolaes Visscher. It is part of a private collection.

**Page 21 (right):** The title pages of a Jewish sermon given in Rhode Island in 1773. Housed in the U.S. Library of Congress in Washington, D.C.

**Page 22:** Pictured is the Royal Charter of Rhode Island and Providence Plantations, issued in 1663, by King Charles II. This charter is housed in the Rhode Island Historical Society in Providence, Rhode Island.

**Page 31:** The Acts & Resolves of the Rhode Island General Assembly, 1783-1784, Volume 23, page 124, authorized the "manumission of Negroes, Mulattos & Others and for the gradual abolition of slavery." This document is part of a special collection of the Rhode Island State Archives in Providence, Rhode Island.

**Page 33:** An eighteenth-century bureau table made by the carpentry shop of Rhode Islander John Townsend. This piece is now in the collection of the Museum of Fine Arts in Houston, Texas.

**Page 36:** Accounting page of a notebook written in the hand of John Stevens, a colonial stonemason working in Newport, Rhode Island, in 1728. This notebook and a variety of other business records from the colonial period can be found at the Newport Historical Society in Newport, Rhode Island.

**Page 39:** The title page to the pamphlet *The Rights of the Colonies Examined*. Stephen Hopkins wrote the pamphlet in December 1765, shortly after the passage of the Stamp Act.

**Page 40:** A political cartoon published in Boston newspapers in response to the Stamp Act of 1765. Housed in the U. S. Library of Congress in Washington, D. C.

**Page 42:** Proclamation issued on August 26, 1772, by King George III seeking an award for any persons caught who were responsible for the destruction of the British ship *Gaspee*.

**Page 46:** William Faden created this map, *A Plan for the Town of Newport*, in 1777. It is housed in the U.S. Library of Congress in Washington, D. C.

**Page 48:** Diary entry of Colonel Israel Angell, descendant of Thomas Angell, dated August 22, 1778. Israel Angell was in command of the Second Rhode Island Continental Regiment during the American Revolution (1778-1781). The Israel Angell Papers (MSS 980, Box 1, Folder 1) are housed in the collection of the Rhode Island Historical Society in Providence, Rhode Island.

**Page 49:** John Fielding first published this engraving of General Nathanael Greene in 1785. It later appeared in the book *The American Revolution in Drawings and Prints*. It is housed at the U. S. Library of Congress in Washington, D. C.

**Page 50:** This notice was originally printed in Philadelphia newspapers on May 30, 1787. It is now housed in the U. S. Library of Congress in Washington, D. C.

# INDEX

## About the Author

Joan Axelrod-Contreda is a journalist and author whose personal heroes include Roger Williams and Anne Hutchinson, two of the founders of Rhode Island. She lives in western Massachusetts with her husband and family.

## Photo Credits

Cover, North Wind Picture Archives; p. 1, Smithsonian Institution, Washington, D. C., USA/Bridgeman Art Library; pp. 8, 50, 40 Library of Congress, Prints and Photographs Division; p. 9 RHi X3 2515 in the collection of the Rhode Island Historical Society; p. 10 (top) Rhode Island State Archives, Rhode Island Colony Records 1646–1669, Deed of Providence; pp. 10 (bottom), 25 © Bettmann/Corbis; p. 12 © Getty Images; p. 14 Rhode Island State Archives, Records of the Island of Rhode Island, 1638–1644; p. 15 © The New York Public Library/Art Resource, NY; p. 17 © Private Collection/Bridgeman Art Library; pp. 21 (right), 49, 50 Library of Congress, Rare Book and Special Collections Division; p. 21 (left) Library of Congress, Hebraic Section; p. 22 Rhode Island State Archives, King Charles II Royal Charter; p. 29 © Courtesy Nicholson Whaling Collection, Providence Public Library; p. 31 Acts & Resolves of the Rhode Island General Assembly, 1783–1784, Vol. 23 p. 124, Rhode Island State Archives; p. 33 © Museum of Fine Arts, Houston, Texas, USA, the Bayou Bend Collection, gift of Miss Ima Hogg/Bridgeman Art Library; p. 34 © Brown University Library; p. 36 Newport Historical Society; p. 42 (bottom) Rhode Island State Archives, *Gaspee* Papers 1772–1773, *Gaspee* Commission; p. 42 (top) RHi X5 10, Brownell, Charles DeWolf, *The Burning of the Gaspee, 1772*, Rhode Island, 1892, oil on canvas painting, Museum Collection: 1893.10.1. in the collection of the Rhode Island Historical Society; p. 48 RHi X4 241, in the collection of the Rhode Island Historical Society; p. 46 Library of Congress, Geography and Map Division.

Editor: Joann Jovinelly